THE FLEET

Miles Cowsill and John Hendy

© 1997 Ferry Publications
PO Box 9
Narberth
Pembrokeshire SA68 0YT

Tel 01834 891461
Fax 01834 891463

ISBN 1 871947 44 8

In 1946 Sten Olsson purchased his first ship, a 21 year old former Norwegian whaler which was converted into a three masted schooner and named *Dan*, after his son. In the following years a series of second hand coastal cargo vessels was secured and during the fifties, purpose-built tonnage came and went in line with Olsson's business philosophy of, 'buy cheap, sell dear.'

Stena AB was formed in 1963 and marked a major change in the direction of the company. The possibility of day shopping excursions to Denmark had been considered for some time and Skagenlinjen AB was formed using chartered tonnage and the two elderly passenger vessels *Skagen I* and *Skagen II*. Such was the success of their services that orders were soon placed for two, small, diesel ferries, named *Poseidon* (which gave services from Gothenburg to both Frederikshavn and Skagen) and *Afrodide*, which, ran on a variety of routes including that from the southern Swedish port of Malmo to Kastrup.

During the mid-sixties, Stena operated a large number of short-sea crossings linking Sweden and Denmark all of which were aimed at the shopping excursion trade. A service linking Stockholm with the Aland Islands also commenced in 1965 and was successfully operated for ten years. Initially using the former German vessel *Wappen*, she was followed by the *Poseidon* after her services to Skagen were abandoned in 1965.

The time was ripe for improved services between Gothenburg and Frederikshavn when in June 1965, the first of Stena's ro-ro passenger ferries were delivered from La Trait in France. The *Stena Danica* was the first ship to carry the distinctive 'Stena' prefix to her name but as trade had not developed in the way that been hoped for, the second ship, *Stena Nordica*, was seasonally employed between Tilbury and Calais where she was marketed as, 'The Londoner.' The route proved to be too long but for the first time ever, entertainment was given on board a cross Channel ferry and patrons of the new service experienced their first taste of the Scandinavian ferry concept.

The *Stena Nordica* was offered for sale at the close of the 1965 season but was chartered instead to the Caledonian Steam Packet Company (Irish Services) Ltd. to support their link between Stranraer and Larne. This was the first of many charters and over the following years, ships with the familiar Stena funnel became increasingly common in British waters. The Tilbury - Calais link was operated by Sessan Line's *Prinsessan Christina* during the 1966 season.

In April 1967 the new *Stena Germanica*, followed very briefly early in 1968 by the much delayed *Stena Brittanica*, was delivered to operate a new overnight service linking Gothenburg and the German port of Kiel. The delay and subsequent sale of the *Stena Britannica* saw Stena introduce the five year old former Swedish Lloyd car ferry *Saga*, lately from the Gothenburg - Tilbury link. Renamed *Stena Atlantica*, the vessel commenced a year of operations to Kiel in March 1972. During that year, a day service to Korsor was commenced by utilising the vessel laying-over in Kiel but as the ships grew larger, so they were unable to enter Korsor harbour and the link ceased. In September that year the *Stena Atlantica* also inaugurated an unsuccessful day sailing from Kiel to Copenhagen.

Legislation covering manning levels on all Swedish registered ships was imposed during 1969 as a result of which many of the smaller vessels were disposed of and replaced by larger ferries. A new *Stena Danica* was built in Bremerhaven and two new ferries named *Stena Olympica* and *Stena Scandinavica* (the latter still in service as Irish Ferries' *Saint Killian II*) were promptly ordered from Yugoslavian builders to operate the overnight Kiel link. The arrival in service of the 'Scandinavica' in July 1973 saw the original Kiel ship (*Stena*

Stena Invicta *(Miles Cowsill)*

Germanica) switched to the Stockholm - Aland Islands service on which she offered overnight accommodation for the first time.

Two more Yugoslavian-built vessels (the *Stena Jutlandica* and *Stena Danica* (III) - delivered as the *Stena Nordica* (III)) entered service on the Frederikshavn crossing in June 1973 and June 1974. Two years later they were both modified and received an extra lorry deck which raised their freight carrying capacity by 70%.

The purely ro-ro market was not forgotten and in 1970 - 72, the *Stena Carrier*, *Stena Trailer*, *Stubbenkammer* and *Anderida* (the latter two sold during the course of construction) were all built in Norway. The first two eventually became Sealink's *Ulidia* and *Dalriada* (Stranraer - Larne route) while the *Anderida* initially worked the Sealink train ferry service from Dover to Dunkerque.

Three Dutch-built ro-ro freighters - the *Stena Sailer*, *Stena Seatrader* and *Stena Shipper* entered service in 1973 for the blossoming charter market.

In 1974 - 75, four more identical sisters came from Bremerhaven shipbuilders, again for the charter market. These were the *Stena Nautica*, *Stena Normandica*, *Stena Nordica* and *Stena Atlantica* two of which (the second and third in the series) served extensive periods in service around the British Isles as Sealink's *St. Brendan* (Fishguard -Rosslare) and the Belgian Government's *Reine Astrid*. The other two were immediately chartered to Canadian owners.

No fewer than six more ro-ro vessels of the 'Stena Seaporter' class, three from Germany and three from Austria, were ordered in a six month period during 1974 - 75. The first two German ships were named *Bison* and *Buffalo* by their charterers (later purchasers) and remain in service for Pandoro today. The third was the *Union Melbourne* which later joined its sisters as the *Puma*.

Stena Challenger *(FotoFlite)*

The three Austrian ships were the *Stena Tender*, *Stena Timer* and *Stena Topper*. All sorts of problems were experienced building them in sections on the Danube near Vienna before towing their component parts down the river for completion in Romania. The first ship is today also part of the P&O Irish Sea operation and serves as their *Leopard*, the second was initially P&O's *Jaguar* while the third became Sealink's *Darnia* (Stranraer - Larne route), later being converted to ro-pax mode with 400 passengers.

Towards the close of 1975 three 'Stena Searunner' class freighters were ordered from the Far East to be followed a year later by an order for six more. There are plenty of these vessels in service around the British Isles today - P&O North Sea Ferries have four of them based at Felixstowe while P&O Ferrymasters operate the *Elk* from Middlesbrough to Gothenburg. To meet the growing demands of the ro-ro industry, the highly versatile Searunner class have been lengthened, raised or widened thereby increasing their capacity.

In April 1979, Stena Line introduced a new service linking Oslo and Frederikshavn. This immediately proved to be extremely popular and offset the loss of the Aland link four years previously. The ship which operated the route for nine seasons was the first named *Stena Saga* which, as the *Patricia*, had formerly operated Swedish Lloyd's car ferry link between Southampton and Bilbao.

The year 1980 saw Stena Line absorb their rivals on the Gothenburg - Frederikshavn service. Sessan Line offered an 'up market' service and had just built two new vessels for the link. The first was the *Kronprinsessan Victoria* (later known in the UK as the Harwich - Hook vessel, *Stena Europe*) while the second (*Prinsessan Birgitta*), which was still fitting out at the time of the 'merger,' soon became Harwich - Hook's *St. Nicholas* and later the Southampton - Cherbourg ferry, *Stena Normandy*. The 'Victoria' was used on the Gothenburg - Kiel overnight service for seven years before later switching to the Oslo link.

Stena's own day vessels were then under construction in Dunkerque (the *Stena Danica* and *Stena Jutlandica*) while four night vessels, for delivery in 1983 - 84 were ordered from Poland. Strikes in the Gdynia and Gdansk shipyards saw the delayed entry of the first two and the *Stena Germanica* and *Stena Scandinavica* eventually entered service some four years late in April 1987 and February 1988. The other two hulls were later sold.

The fourth-named *Stena Danica* eventually entered service in February 1983 to be followed by the *Stena Jutlandica* (II) in April.

In August 1982, Stena Line took over the operation of the Varberg - Grena route and began to operate Lion Ferry as a subsidiary company. An additional link from Halmstad - Grena was added during 1988 using the former *Stena Saga*, now renamed *Lion Queen* after having been replaced on the Gothenburg - Oslo link in May 1988 by the *Stena Saga* (II) ex. *Kronprinsessan Victoria*. The following year, the *Lion Queen* was transferred to the Helsingborg - Grena route which closed in October 1989. Thereafter she became the *Crown Princess Victoria* for the short-lived BC Stena Line service between Canada and the USA.

In spring 1983, the Frederikshavn route was expanded with the addition of a nightly call at the Norwegian port of Moss. This continued until 1996 when the *Stena Nordica* (VI) was transferred to Lion Ferry's Halmstad - Grena route and renamed *Lion King*.

With competition building in the domestic Scandinavian sphere of operations, it was only natural that Stena Line should now seek to broaden its core ferry business and look elsewhere for improved profits.

In 1988, Stena AB successfully purchased the British Columbia Steamship Ltd. and restyled it BC Stena Line. The venture was not a commercial success and sadly closed in

1990.

The next acquisition occurred in April 1989 when Stena AB acquired Crown Line (Stoomvaart Maatschappij Zeeland) from the Dutch Government thereby giving them a strong base from which to further expand into the very competitive North Sea market. The operation of the purpose-built ferry *Koningin Beatrix* was soon complemented by the former Silja Line vessel *Silvia Regina* which was renamed *Stena Britannica* in June 1991. She replaced the *St. Nicholas/ Stena Normandy* which, in turn, was transferred to Southampton.

The 'Britannica' was later moved to the Oslo service in March 1994 when she exchanged routes with the *Stena Saga* (II) whose name she duly adopted. The former 'Saga' became the *Stena Europe*.

A further purchase occurred early in 1989 when Stena acquired 8% of Sea Containers' shares on the New York stock exchange. After a protracted hostile take-over bid, the following year eventually saw the £259 million purchase of Sealink British Ferries, along with five routes and the ports of Harwich (Parkeston Quay - which was sold in August 1997), Fishguard, Holyhead and Stranraer.

The link between Southampton and Cherbourg, using the *Stena Normandy*, was added in July 1991 but increasing competition in the Western Channel saw its demise in November 1996.

In preparation for the opening of the Channel Tunnel, Folkestone - Boulogne became an early route casualty and closed in December 1991 after almost 150 years of operation. An additional route was acquired in spring 1992 when the Dieppe - Newhaven service was purchased from French operators Sealink SNAT. They had operated the loss-making link alone since Sea Containers had withdrawn in January 1985 and their *Versailles*, ex. *Stena Danica* (III) became the British crewed *Stena Londoner*.

The historic North Channel link between Stranraer and Larne also succumbed, in favour of a new service to Belfast, in November 1995.

With the introduction of the third HSS, the *Stena Discovery*, on the Hook of Holland - Harwich route in June 1997, the *Stena Europe* (ex. *Kronprinsessan Victoria* and *Stena Saga*) transferred to the third Lion Ferry link between Karlskrona and Gdynia as their *Lion Europe*. Running partner *Koningin Beatrix* was duly placed on the Fishguard - Rosslare link in place of the *Stena Felicity* which was returned to her owners, Gotland Line.

During 1996 and in the early part of 1997, it was possible to cross the English Channel from Dover to Calais in the third-named *Stena Danica* (by then named *SeaFrance Monet*) of 1974 and return in the second-named *Stena Jutlandica* (renamed *Stena Empereur*) of 1983 - second and third generation ferries from Stena Line's premier route linking its historic base at Gothenburg to the Danish port of Frederikshavn.

The nine years between both vessels gave ample indication just how much traffic on the cross Kattegatt route had grown in that short period. Today the emphasis is on speed and firstly the 78 metre *Stena Lynx II* followed more recently by the new HSS 900 craft *Stena Carisma* can ship up to 900 passengers and 210 cars in as little as two hours. Freight is accommodated on board the route's extremely flexible modern ro-pax vessel, *Stena Jutlandica* (III) while the faithful *Stena Danica* (IV) continues to offer a total range of facilities for all classes and types of conventional traffic.

From this brief resume of Stena Line's ferry activities, it is plain to see to what extent the ferry industry has relied on the line's spare or charter tonnage. This, however, is only half the story and there are many more instances, too numerous to mention here, where brief

Stena Jutlandica *(Stena Line)*

and short-term charters have allowed most UK - Continent and UK - Ireland routes to continue operational during periods of breakdown or short fall of tonnage.

In recent years technology has allowed all modes of transport - with the exception of sea travel - to reach their destinations in quicker times. At last, the recent revolution in the fast ferry industry has finally allowed ferry traffic to benefit in terms of speed.

Stena's entry into fast ferry travel has been as sudden as it has been dramatic. They leased their first InCat 74 metre catamaran from Buquebus SA of Montevideo, Uruguay, and named *Stena Sea Lynx* introduced the craft onto the Holyhead - Dun Laoghaire route in July 1993. Its success saw the addition of the 78 metre *Stena Sea Lynx II* in the following June after which the first vessel was transferred to Fishguard's southern corridor. Both craft quickly captured 40% of the car traffic on their respective routes and showed that the customers did not object to paying a premium for a speed return.

Stena's decision to proceed with an untried design represented a tremendous leap of faith on the part of the company. With the three gigantic HSS 1500 craft now in operation from Holyhead to Dun Laoghaire (*Stena Explorer*), Stranraer to Belfast (*Stena Voyager*) and Harwich to the Hook of Holland (*Stena Discovery*), Stena are as far ahead of the field as it is possible to be. Tonnage-wise, the craft were five times larger than the largest existing fast ferry.

Investment in the three HSS craft and allied shore facilities amounted to £300 million. Each HSS is powered by four gas turbine engines via four waterjets producing 100,000 horse power (the same as a jumbo jet) which drive them at a top speed in excess of 40 knots. The craft measure 126 metres by 40 metres and can accommodate up to 1,500 passengers, 375 cars (or 120 cars and 50 coaches or 50 lorries) - the first high speed ferries to carry freight.

In 1995, Stena announced the construction of two new classes of freight ships that could operate opposite the HSS craft if necessary, providing enough freight space and offering passenger accommodation if extra capacity was required.

The first of the new class of vessels is the 'Stena Seapacer' class which are presently being built in Puerto Real in Spain. They will accommodate about 440 passengers, 2,500 metres of freight and operate at speeds of up to 22 knots. Four of these ro-pax ships are on order and the first two are due in service later this year. At the time of writing there was a degree of speculation concerning the placement of at least one of them on the Harwich - Hook of Holland link.

The second group of no fewer than seven ro-ro ships are called the 'Stena 4-Runner' class and are presently under construction at Viareggio in Italy. Capacity will be for twelve drivers and 2,715 lane metres of freight while speed is again, an impressive 22 knots.

A glimpse at the line's order book and recent investments provides ample evidence that Stena are preparing to meet the new millennium with a fleet of thoroughly modern vessels, many of which we may expect to see in service around the coasts of the United Kingdom.

When, in 1939, Sten A. Olsson founded a scrap metal business in his native Sweden, he could have had no notion that within sixty years the company which bore his name would have grown and expanded to become the force which is now evident in metals, international trading in oil, steel and recycled paper. The subject of this publication is the Stena ferry division which is just one unit of a far larger business. Stena Line claims that theirs is the world's largest ferry company for international traffic. Their network consists of 14 ferry routes in north western Europe: in Scandinavia, the Baltic Sea, the English Channel and the Irish Sea.

In conclusion, it is perhaps time to recall Dan Sten Olsson's words that Stena continues to fulfil three important criteria - "respect for man, respect for money and, the will to be best at what we are doing."

The **Stena Danica** arriving at Gothenburg from Denmark. *(John Hendy)*

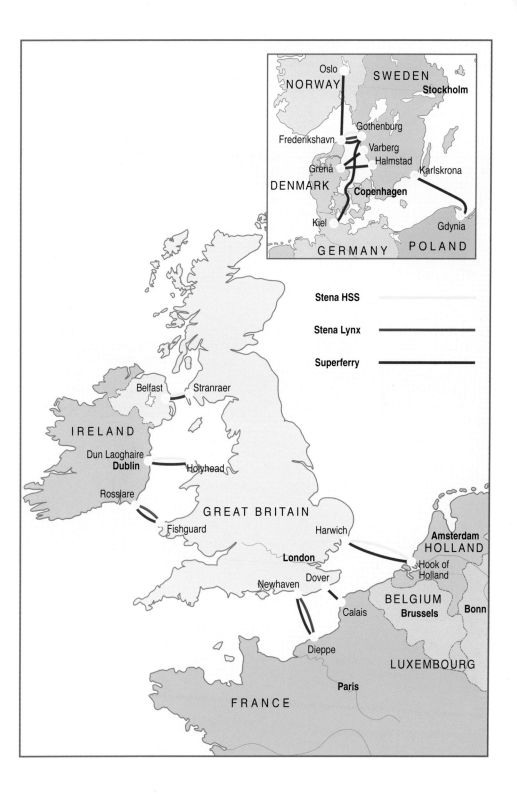

Stena HSS

Stena Lynx

Superferry

Stena Line

STENA ANTRIM

Year Built/Year Refitted	1981
Yard and Country	Harland & Wolff, Northern Ireland
Class of Ship	Multi-purpose ferry
Owner	City Leasing Ltd
Flag	British
Port of Registry	Stranraer
Route Operated	Newhaven - Dieppe
Disposition Format	Leased, option to buy (earliest): 1 Feb 2001
Length	130m
Beam	22m
Draught	5.0m
Deadweight	1,730 tons
Gross tonnage	12,711 tons
Passenger Capacity	1,300
Private Cars Capacity	290
Freight Capacity	750 lane metres/50 x 16 m trailers
No. Berths	-
Type of Engine	2xPielstick
Propulsion	Propeller
Speed in Knots/kW/Hp	19.5/15,294/20,800
Former Name	*St. Christopher*

Year Built/Year Refitted	1981
Yard and Country	Harland & Wolff, Northern Ireland
Class of Ship	Multi-purpose ferry
Owner	City Leasing Ltd
Flag	British
Port of Registry	Stranraer
Route Operated	Stranraer - Belfast
Disposition Format	Leased, option to buy (earliest): 1 Feb 2001
Length	130m
Beam	22m
Draught	5.0m
Deadweight	1,730 tons
Gross tonnage	12,619 tons
Passenger Capacity	1,000
Private Cars Capacity	280
Freight Capacity	675 lane metres
No. Berths	-
Type of Engine	2xPielstick
Propulsion	Propeller
Speed in Knots/kW/Hp	19.5/15,294/20,800
Former Name	*St. David*

STENA CALEDONIA

Miles Cowsill

STENA CAMBRIA

Year Built/Year Refitted	1980
Yard and Country	Harland & Wolff, Northern Ireland
Class of Ship	Multi-purpose ferry
Owner	R B Equipment Leasing
Flag	British
Port of Registry	London
Route Operated	Dover - Calais
Disposition Format	Leased, option to buy (earliest): 1 Dec 2001
Length	130m
Beam	22m
Draught	5.0m
Deadweight	1,708 tons
Gross tonnage	12,705 tons
Passenger Capacity	1,300
Private Cars Capacity	280
Freight Capacity	675 lane metres + 30 cars
No. Berths	-
Type of Engine	2xPielstick
Propulsion	Propeller
Speed in Knots/kW/Hp	19.5/15,294/20,800
Former Name	*St. Anselm*

Stena Line

Year Built/Year Refitted	1997
Yard and Country	West Bygg AS, Norway
Class of Ship	Fast ferry HSS 900
Owner	Stena Line
Flag	Swedish
Port of Registry	Göteborg
Route Operated	Göteborg - Frederikshavn
Disposition Format	-
Length	88m
Beam	30m
Draught	3.9m
Deadweight	
Gross tonnage	480 tons
Passenger Capacity	900
Private Cars Capacity	210
Freight Capacity	170 cars + 10 buses
No. Berths	-
Type of Engine	2xABB-Stal GT 35
Propulsion	2xKaMe Wa 160 Waterjet
Speed in Knots/kW/Hp	40 knots

STENA CARISMA

Stena Line

STENA CARRIER

Year Built/Year Refitted	1978
Yard and Country	Hyundai Heavy Industries, S. Korea
Class of Ship	Freight ferry
Owner	Stena Line
Flag	Cayman Islands
Port of Registry	Georgetown
Route Operated	Göteborg - Travemünde
Disposition Format	Owned, remaining depr. period: 6 years
Length	156m
Beam	21m
Draught	7.3m
Deadweight	8,698 tons
Gross tonnage	13,117 tons
Passenger Capacity	12
Private Cars Capacity	-
Freight Capacity	1,700 lane metres
No. Berths	12
Type of Engine	2xNKK-Pielstick
Propulsion	Propeller
Speed in Knots/kW/Hp	18/11,475/15,600
Year Built/Year Refitted	1991
Former names	*Imparca Express I, Imparca Miami, Jolly Bruno, Jolly Smeraldo*

Miles Cowsill

Yard and Country	Fosen, Norway
Class of Ship	Ro-pax ferry
Owner	Stena Sphere
Flag	British
Port of Registry	Dover
Route Operated	Holyhead - Dublin
Disposition Format	Chartered, charter expires: 24 May 2001
Length	157m
Beam	24m
Draught	5.5m
Deadweight	4,650 tons
Gross tonnage	18,523 tons
Passenger Capacity	500
Private Cars Capacity	480
Freight Capacity	1,200 lane metres
No. Berths	10
Type of Engine	2xSulzer
Propulsion	Propeller
Speed in Knots/kW/Hp	18/10,555/14,400

STENA CHALLENGER

Miles Cowsill

STENA DANICA

Year Built/Year Refitted	1983/1995
Yard and Country	Chantiers du Nord, France
Class of Ship	Multi-purpose ferry
Owner	Stena Line
Flag	Swedish
Port of Registry	Göteborg
Route Operated	Göteborg - Frederikshavn
Disposition Format	Owned, remaining depr. period: 11 years
Length	155m
Beam	29m
Draught	6.3m
Deadweight	2,953 tons
Gross tonnage	28,727 tons
Passenger Capacity	2,274
Private Cars Capacity	555
Freight Capacity	1,640 lane metres/76 trucks + 36 cars
No. Berths	74
Type of Engine	4xCCM Sulzer
Propulsion	Propeller
Speed in Knots/kW/Hp	19.5/25,612/34,800

Stena Line

Year Built/Year Refitted	1997
Yard and Country	Finnyards, Finland
Class of Ship	Fast ferry HSS 1500
Owner	Stena AB Group
Flag	Netherlands
Port of Registry	Hoek van Holland
Route Operated	Hoek van Holland - Harwich
Disposition Format	
Length	127m
Beam	40m
Draught	4.8m
Deadweight	1,500 tons
Gross tonnage	19,638 tons
Passenger Capacity	1,500
Private Cars Capacity	375
Freight Capacity	50 x 16 m trailers + 100 cars
No. Berths	-
Type of Engine	2xGE LM 2500 + 2xGE LM 1600
Propulsion	Waterjet
Speed in Knots/kW/Hp	40/73, 529/100,000

STENA DISCOVERY

John Hendy

Year built/year refitted	1983/1996
Yard and country	Chantiers du Nord, France
Class of Ship	Multi-purpose ferry
Owner	Stena Line
Flag	British
Port of Registry	London
Route Operated	Dover - Calais
Disposition Format	Owned, remaining depr. period: 11 years
Length	155m
Beam	29m
Draught	6.3m
Deadweight	2,459 tons
Gross tonnage	28,559 tons
Passenger capacity	2.036
Private Cars Capacity	550
Freight Capacity	1,312 lane metres, 86 x 16 m trailers
No. Berths	82
Type of Engine	4xCCM Sulzer
Propulsion	Propeller
Speed in Knots/kW/Hp	19.5/25,612/34,800
Former name	*Stena Jutlandica*

STENA EMPEREUR

Miles Cowsill

Year built/year refitted	1996
Yard and country	Finnyards, Finland
Class of Ship	HSS 1500 fast ferry
Owner	Stena Sphere
Flag	British
Port of Registry	London
Route Operated	Holyhead - Dun Laoghaire
Disposition Format	Chartered, charter expires: 16 Feb 2001
Length	127m
Beam	40m
Draught	4.6m
Deadweight	1,500 tons
Gross tonnage	19,638 tons
Passenger capacity	1,500
Private Cars Capacity	375
Freight Capacity	50 x 16 m trailers + 100 cars
No. Berths	-
Type of Engine	2xGE LM 1 500+2xGE LM 1 600
Propulsion	Waterjet
Speed in Knots/kW/Hp	40/73,529/100,000

STENA EXPLORER

STENA FANTASIA

John Hendy

Year built/year refitted	1980/1991
Yard and country	Kockums AB, Sweden
Class of Ship	Multi-purpose ferry
Owner	Ixora Ltd
Flag	Bahamas
Port of Registry	Nassau
Route Operated	Dover - Calais
Disposition Format	Leased, option to buy (earliest): 31 March 2005
Length	164m
Beam	28m
Draught	6.5m
Deadweight	3,100 tons
Gross tonnage	25,122 tons
Passenger capacity	1,800
Private Cars Capacity	550
Freight Capacity	1,000 lane metres + 60 cars
No. Berths	-
Type of Engine	2xSulzer
Propulsion	Propeller
Speed in Knots/kW/Hp	19/13,015/17,700
Former names	*Scandinavia, Tzarevetz, Fiesta, Fantasia*

Year built/year refitted	1977
Yard and country	Hyundai Heavy Industries, S. Korea
Class of Ship	Freight ferry
Owner	Stena Line
Flag	Swedish
Port of Registry	Göteborg
Route Operated	Göteborg - Travemünde
Disposition Format	Owned, remaining depr. period: 1 year
Length	156m
Beam	20m
Draught	7.3m
Deadweight	8,800 tons
Gross tonnage	13,134 tons
Passenger capacity	12
Private Cars Capacity	-
Freight Capacity	1,700 lane metres/117 trailers
No. Berths	12
Type of Engine	2xNKK-SEMT Pielstick
Propulsion	Propeller
Speed in Knots/kW/Hp	18/11,475/15,600
Former names	*Merzario Ausonia, Jolly Giallo, Jolly Turchese*

STENA FREIGHTER

Miles Cowsill

STENA GALLOWAY

Year Built/Year Refitted	1980
Yard and Country	Harland & Wolff, Northern Ireland
Class of Ship	Multi-purpose ferry
Owner	IBOS Finance Ltd
Flag	British
Port of Registry	Stranraer
Route Operated	Stranraer - Belfast
Disposition Format	Leased, option to buy (earliest): 1 Dec 2000
Length	130m
Beam	22m
Draught	4.7m
Deadweight	1,688 tons
Gross tonnage	12,175 tons
Passenger Capacity	1,000
Private Cars Capacity	280
Freight Capacity	675 lane metres + 30 cars
No. Berths	-
Type of Engine	2xPielstick
Propulsion	Propeller
Speed in Knots/kW/Hp	19/11.765/16,000
Former name	*Galloway Princess*

Year Built/Year Refitted	1987/1996
Yard and Country	Stocznia Gdansk, Poland
Class of Ship	Multi-purpose ferry
Owner	Stena Line
Flag	Swedish
Port of Registry	Göteborg
Route Operated	Göteborg - Kiel
Disposition Format	Owned, remaining depr. period: 15 years
Length	175m
Beam	29m
Draught	6.7m
Deadweight	4,500 tons
Gross tonnage	38,772 tons
Passenger Capacity	2,400
Private Cars Capacity	550
Freight Capacity	1,320 lane metres/80 x 16 m + 55 cars
No. Berths	2,440
Type of Engine	4xSulzer
Propulsion	Propeller
Speed in Knots/kW/Hp	20/30,617/41,600

STENA GERMANICA

Miles Cowsill

STENA GOTHICA

Year Built/Year Refitted	1975/1990
Yard and Country	Framnaes Mek, Vaerkstad, Norway
Class of Ship	Freight Ferry
Owner	Stena Line
Flag	Swedish
Port of Registry	Göteborg
Route Operated	Göteborg - Harwich
Disposition Format	Owned, remaining depr. period: 6 years
Length	189m
Beam	21m
Draught	7.0m
Deadweight	12,211 tons
Gross tonnage	14,406 tons
Passenger Capacity	12
Private Cars Capacity	280
Freight Capacity	2,000 lane metres
No. Berths	12
Type of Engine	2xPielstick
Propulsion	Propeller
Speed in Knots/kW/Hp	16/8,832/12,000
Former names	*Melbourne Trader, Monawar L*

Year Built/Year Refitted	1985/1996
Yard and Country	Nakskov Skibsvaerft, Denmark
Class of Ship	Multi-purpose ferry
Owner	Stena Line
Flag	British
Port of Registry	Dover
Route Operated	Dover - Calais
Disposition Format	Owned, remaining depr. period: 14 years
Length	137m
Beam	25m
Draught	5.7m
Deadweight	2,390 tons
Gross tonnage	19,763 tons
Passenger Capacity	1,750
Private Cars Capacity	320
Freight Capacity	510 lane metres + 145 cars
No. Berths	-
Type of Engine	2xMAN/B&W
Propulsion	Propeller
Speed in Knots/kW/Hp	17.5/12,471/17,000
Former name	*Peder Paas*

STENA INVICTA

Miles Cowsill

STENA JUTLANDICA

Year Built/Year Refitted	1996
Yard and Country	Van der Giessen-de Noord, Netherlands
Class of Ship	Ro-pax ferry
Owner	Stena Sphere
Flag	Swedish
Port of Registry	Göteborg
Route Operated	Göteborg - Frederikshavn
Disposition Format	Leased, option to buy (earliest): 20 Dec 1999
Length	184m
Beam	28m
Draught	6.0m
Deadweight	6,300 tons
Gross tonnage	29,691 tons
Passenger Capacity	1,500
Private Cars Capacity	550
Freight Capacity	2,100 lane metres + 130 cars
No. Berths	197
Type of Engine	4xMAN
Propulsion	Propeller
Speed in Knots/kW/Hp	21.5/25,920/32,300

Year Built/Year Refitted	1986/1994
Yard and Country	Van der Giessen-de-Noord, Netherlands
Class of Ship	Multi-purpose ferry
Owner	Stena Line
Flag	British
Port of Registry	London
Route Operated	Fishguard - Rosslare
Disposition Format	Owned, remaining depr. period: 13 years
Length	162m
Beam	28m
Draught	6.2m
Deadweight	3,632 tons
Gross tonnage	31,189 tons
Passenger Capacity	1,800
Private Cars Capacity	500
Freight Capacity	900 lane metres
No. Berths	1,300
Type of Engine	4xMAN
Propulsion	Propeller
Speed in Knots/kW/Hp	20/19,360/26,400

KONINGIN BEATRIX

Miles Cowsill

STENA LYNX

Year Built/Year Refitted	1993
Yard and Country	InCat, Australia
Class of Ship	Fast ferry
Owner	Buquebus International
Flag	Bahamas
Port of Registry	Nassau
Route Operated	Fishguard - Rosslare
Disposition Format	Chartered, charter expires: 30 Sept 1998
Length	75m
Beam	27m
Draught	3.2m
Deadweight	200 tons
Gross tonnage	3,231 tons
Passenger Capacity	430
Private Cars Capacity	88
Freight Capacity	-
No. Berths	-
Type of Engine	4xRuston
Propulsion	Waterjet
Speed in Knots/kW/Hp	37/16,182/22,000
Former name	*Stena Sea Lynx*

Year Built/Year Refitted	1994
Yard and Country	InCat, Australia
Class of Ship	Fast ferry
Owner	Buquebus International
Flag	Bahamas
Port of Registry	Nassau
Route Operated	Göteborg - Frederikshavn
Disposition Format	Chartered, charter expires: 1 Nov 1997
Length	78m
Beam	27m
Draught	3.4m
Deadweight	267 tons
Gross tonnage	3,989 tons
Passenger Capacity	612
Private Cars Capacity	135
Freight Capacity	-
No. Berths	-
Type of Engine	4xCaterpillar
Propulsion	Waterjet
Speed in Knots/kW/Hp	37/17,296/23,500
Former name	*Stena Sea Lynx II*

STENA LYNX II

John Hendy

STENA LYNX III

Year Built/Year Refitted	1996
Yard and Country	InCat, Australia
Class of Ship	Fast ferry
Owner	AFFL, American Fast Ferries Ltd
Flag	Bahamas
Port of Registry	Nassau
Route Operated	Newhaven - Dieppe
Disposition Format	Chartered, charter expires: 1 Nov 1998
Length	79m
Beam	23m
Draught	2.4m
Deadweight	340 tons
Gross tonnage	4,113 tons
Passenger Capacity	670
Private Cars Capacity	148/10 coaches + 28 cars
Freight Capacity	-
No. Berths	-
Type of Engine	4xRuston
Propulsion	Waterjet
Speed in Knots/kW/Hp	35/22,000/29,900

Year Built/Year Refitted	1981/1995
Yard and Country	Wärtsilä, Finland
Class of Ship	Multi-purpose ferry
Owner	Stena Sphere
Flag	Swedish
Port of Registry	Stockholm
Route Operated	Oslo - Frederikshavn
Disposition Format	Chartered, charter expires: 30 April 1998
Length	166m
Beam	28m
Draught	6.8m
Deadweight	3,799 tons
Gross tonnage	33,750 tons
Passenger Capacity	2,000
Private Cars Capacity	510
Freight Capacity	1,050 lane metres
No. Berths	1,601
Type of Engine	4xWärtsilä - Pielstick
Propulsion	Propeller
Speed in Knots/kW/Hp	22/22,963/31,200
Former names	*Silvia Regina, Stena Britannica*

STENA SAGA

STENA SCANDINAVICA

Year Built/Year Refitted	1988/1996
Yard and Country	Stocznia Gdansk, Poland
Class of Ship	Multi-purpose ferry
Owner	Stena Line
Flag	Swedish
Port of Registry	Göteborg
Route Operated	Göteborg - Kiel
Disposition Format	Owned, remaining depr. period: 16 years
Length	175m
Beam	29m
Draught	6.7m
Deadweight	3,415 tons
Gross tonnage	38,756 tons
Passenger Capacity	2,400
Private Cars Capacity	550
Freight Capacity	1,320 lane metres
No. Berths	2,454
Type of Engine	4xSulzer
Propulsion	Propeller
Speed in Knots/kW/Hp	20/30,617/41,600

Year Built/Year Refitted	1973/1996
Yard and Country	A. Vuyk & Zonen, Netherlands
Class of Ship	Freight ferry
Owner	Stena Line
Flag	Swedish
Port of Registry	Göteborg
Route Operated	Göteborg - Frederikshavn
Disposition Format	Owned, remaining depr. period: 1 year
Length	142m
Beam	19m
Draught	4.6m
Deadweight	2,964 tons
Gross tonnage	7,504 tons
Passenger Capacity	65
Private Cars Capacity	-
Freight Capacity	773 lane metres
No. Berths	32
Type of Engine	4xStork Werkspoor
Propulsion	Propeller
Speed in Knots/kW/Hp	16.5/5,299/7,200
Former names	*Seatrader, Stena Searider, Searider, Stena Searider, Trucker*

STENA SCANRAIL

Philippe Holthof

STENA SEARIDER

Year Built/Year Refitted	1969/1995
Yard and Country	Wärtsilä, Finland
Class of Ship	Freight ferry
Owner	Stena Line
Flag	Swedish
Port of Registry	Göteborg
Route Operated	Hoek van Holland - Harwich
Disposition Format	Owned, remaining depr. period: 8 years
Length	179m
Beam	25m
Draught	5.5m
Deadweight	7,034 tons
Gross tonnage	21,019 tons
Passenger Capacity	120
Private Cars Capacity	-
Freight Capacity	2,390 lane metres
No. Berths	105
Type of Engine	2xPielstick
Propulsion	Propeller
Speed in Knots/kW/Hp	17/9,936/13,500

Former names   *Finncarrier, Polaris, Scandinavia, Scandinavia Link, Stena Searider, Searider, Norse Mersey*

Year Built/Year Refitted	1973
Yard and Country	Nakskov Skibsvaerft, Denmark
Class of Ship	Freight ferry
Owner	Stena Line
Flag	Dutch
Port of Registry	Hoek van Holland
Route Operated	Hoek van Holland - Harwich
Disposition Format	Owned, remaining depr. period: 3 years
Length	183m
Beam	22m
Draught	6.1m
Deadweight	5,737 tons
Gross tonnage	17,991 tons
Passenger Capacity	221
Private Cars Capacity	-
Freight Capacity	2,100 lane metres
No. Berths	221
Type of Engine	4xPielstick
Propulsion	Propeller
Speed in Knots/kW/Hp	17.5/10,500/14,000
Former names	*Svealand, Svealand av Malmo, Svea Link*

STENA SEATRADER

Miles Cowsill

STENA VOYAGER

Year Built/Year Refitted	1996
Yard and Country	Finnyards, Finland
Class of Ship	HSS 1500 fast ferry
Owner	Stena Sphere
Flag	British
Port of Registry	London
Route Operated	Stranraer - Belfast
Disposition Format	Chartered, charter expires: 28 June 2001
Length	127m
Beam	40m
Draught	4.6m
Deadweight	1,500 tons
Gross tonnage	19,638 tons
Passenger Capacity	1,500
Private Cars Capacity	375
Freight Capacity	50 x 16 m trailers + 100 cars
No. Berths	-
Type of Engine	2xGE LM 2 500 + 2GE LM 1 600
Propulsion	Waterjet
Speed in Knots/kW/Hp	40/73,529/100,000

Year built/year refitted	1981/1995
Yard and country	Götaverken, Sweden
Class of Ship	Multi-purpose ferry
Owner	Stena Line
Flag	Swedish
Port of Registry	Göteborg
Route Operated	Karlskrona - Gdynia
Disposition Format	Owned, remaining depr. period: 9 years
Length	149m
Beam	27m
Draught	6.1m
Deadweight	2.366 tons
Gross tonnage	24,828 tons
Passenger capacity	2,076
Private Cars Capacity	456
Freight Capacity	1,692 lane metres, 58 trailers
No. Berths	1,332
Type of Engine	4xWärtsilä Vasa
Propulsion	Propeller
Speed in Knots/kW/Hp	19/15,200/20,700
Former names	*Kronprinsessan Victoria, Stena Saga, Stena Europe*

LION EUROPE

LION KING

Year Built/Year Refitted	1979/1989
Yard and Country	Wärtsilä, Finland
Class of Ship	Multi-purpose ferry
Owner	Stena Line
Flag	Swedish
Port of Registry	Halmstad
Route Operated	Halmstad - Grenå
Disposition Format	Owned, remaining depr. period: 7 years
Length	136m
Beam	24m
Draught	5.5m
Deadweight	2,743 tons
Gross tonnage	16,630 tons
Passenger Capacity	1,700
Private Cars Capacity	425
Freight Capacity	630 lane metres
No. Berths	624
Type of Engine	4xSEMT Pielstick
Propulsion	Propeller
Speed in Knots/kW/Hp	19/17,644/24,000
Former names	*Turella, Stena Nordica*

Year Built/Year Refitted	1969/1984
Yard and Country	Aalborg Vaerft, Denmark
Class of Ship	Multi-purpose ferry
Owner	Stena Line
Flag	Swedish
Port of Registry	Göteborg
Route Operated	Varberg - Grenå
Disposition Format	Owned, remaining depr. period: 1 year
Length	123m
Beam	20m
Draught	5.1m
Deadweight	1,787 tons
Gross tonnage	8,909 tons
Passenger Capacity	1,305
Private Cars Capacity	360
Freight Capacity	510 lane metres + 23 cars
No. Berths	144
Type of Engine	8xNohab Polar
Propulsion	Propeller
Speed in Knots/kW/Hp	18/11,776/16,000
Former names	*Prinsessan Christina, Safe Christina, Stena Nordica, Europafarjan I*

LION PRINCE

Notes

Statistics have been supplied by Stena Line and are therefore assumed to be correct. The spelling 'Göteborg' and its Anglicised version, 'Gothenburg' have both been used in this publication. Disposition Format: the abbreviation depr. has been used for depreciation.

Ferry Publications

Ferry Publications was formed in 1988 by Miles Cowsill and John Hendy who had joined together to write and publish their highly successful *Townsend Thoresen Years*. Since then they have produced a continuous stream of titles which have covered most areas of the North Sea, English Channel and Irish Sea. Disenchantment with writing for other magazines led the partners to launch their own quarterly journal, in the summer of 1989. Now firmly established, **European Ferry Scene** has quickly gained praise from both the enthusiast fraternity and the ferry industry alike. For further information and details on current titles of Ferry Publications, please write to: PO Box 9, Narberth, Pembrokeshire, SA68 0YT.

Acknowledgements

Ferry Publications would like to thank Nick Widdows, Michael Speckenbach, Philippe Holthof and Brian Rees (Stena Line UK) for their invaluable help with this publication.

Stena Fantasia *(John Hendy)*